A Historic Tour

of Boalsburg and along Boalsburg Pike to Lemont, Pennsylvania

George Stroup House

by H. Randolph Thomas

LEMONT

© 2020 Horace Randolph Thomas

Printed in the United States of America

All rights reserved. This publication is protected by Copyright, and permission should be obtained from the publisher prior to any prohibited reproduction, storage in a retrieval system, or transmission in any form or by any means, electronic, mechanical, photocopying, recording, or likewise.

Published by Mt. Nittany Press, an imprint of Eifrig Publishing,
PO Box 66, Lemont, PA 16851. www.eifrigpublishing.com

For information regarding permission, write to:

Rights and Permissions Department,
Eifrig Publishing,
PO Box 66, Lemont, PA 16851, USA.
permissions@eifrigpublishing.com, 888-340-6543.

Library of Congress Cataloging-in-Publication Data

A Historic Tour of Boalsburg and along Boalsburg Pike to Lemont, Pennsylvania /

by Horace Randolph Thomas
p. cm.

Paperback: ISBN 978-1-63233-275-2
eBook: ISBN 978-1-63233-276-9

[1. Boalsburg--Pennsylvania 2. Colonial History--Pennsylvania- 3. Centre County (Pa.)--History]
I. Thomas, Horace Randolph. II. Title

24 23 22 21 2020
5 4 3 2 1

Printed in the USA on recycled paper.

TABLE OF CONTENTS

Preface	5
Introduction	7
Building Practices	10
Architectural Styles	13
Boalsburg Tour	16
Oak Hall-Dale's Mills Tour	34
Other Points of Interest	48
Bibliography	49

DEDICATION

*This book is dedicated to my mother and
high school history teacher,
Virginia Thomas,
who taught me the importance and joy of history
at an early age.*

PREFACE

After the economic crisis of the 1780s, Boalsburg began a period of steady growth. Cottage industries grew into numerous mills that were built in Oak Hall along Spring Creek. Some mills produced finished goods like woolen garments and hemp rope, while other mills produced raw products. The surrounding area supported gristmills and flour mills, iron furnaces, iron ore pits, and quarries. The outside income made the two villages very prosperous. The road network made Boalsburg a gateway to Potter's Mills, down Seven Mountains, and on to eastern markets. The volume of wagon traffic through Boalsburg led to many small businesses that catered to waggoneers and travelers. Here waggoneers could get wagons repaired, horses fed and watered, or, if needed, entirely new wagons could be made. The small businesses included blacksmiths, a tanners, carriage shops, and taverns/inns where one could get food, drink, and overnight accommodations. These services attracted local and cross-state stagecoach business. The stagecoach business further attracted tinsmiths, hatters, seamstresses, boot makers, and more that catered specifically to travelers. Boalsburg became an important center of commerce and likely a favored overnight stagecoach stop. The high-water mark for Boalsburg, economically speaking, was around 1830-1835.

By the end of the 19th century, the situation had changed

dramatically. The stagecoach ceased operation about 1855, and the mills in Oak Hall closed around 1850-1875. The wagon traffic through Boalsburg had been significantly reduced, and the railroad had isolated the village. Many of the craftsmen and artisans had either died, were out of business, or had gone elsewhere. The tannery closed around the end of the century, and carriage shops and blacksmith shops would survive only a short time into the 20th century. The only thing that remained from the first half of the 19th century was agriculture. The primary culprits for the region's decline are attributed to the Industrial Revolution and the coming of the railroad.

This book outlines a tour of historical homes, businesses, and historical sites through Boalsburg to Lemont. The tour is straightforward as all sites are visible from the road. The tour is divided into two parts. The first part is a tour through Boalsburg. If desired, this tour can be done on foot. The second part is a tour of the Oak Hall-Dale's Mills area along Boalsburg Pike in route to Lemont. This part of the tour is not suitable for foot traffic as Boalsburg Pike is heavily traveled and there are no shoulders or sidewalks along the road. Both tours can be accomplished in less than 30 minutes.

INTRODUCTION

How many times have you driven by the Benjamin Poultney house without knowing it is one of the oldest houses in Boalsburg? Do you know where the first schoolhouse in Boalsburg is located? How often have you gone out West Main Street in Boalsburg and not realized that the 200-plus-year-old stone house of George Stroup House was even there? Did you know that the house on the Gingrich Property is also more than 200 years old? Have you driven through Oak Hall and wondered what the historical significance of the Irvin Mansion was? Did you know that the Irvin Mill was once a woolen mill? Where is the Albright Church? Have you ever been to Dale's Mills? If you're like me, you've passed these sites perhaps a hundred times without knowing anything about their significance.

In 1765, the provincial land office opened, and a large tract of land was warranted or surveyed in 1766 to Thomas Poultney. He called the tract the Plantation of Harmony. Benjamin Poultney built a log home on the Harmony Plantation tract in 1774. The relationship between Thomas and Benjamin is not known. The settlement immediately west of Harmony Plantation became known as Springfield because of the spring located at the eastern end of Springfield near the present-day Boalsburg Heritage Museum. The spring originates on the north side of Loop Road directly across from the entrance to the present-day Springfield Commons housing development. The stream flows behind what is now the First National Bank.

David Boal, Sr. served the American cause during the Revolutionary War as a Captain. It was the practice at that time for the States to repay soldiers for their service during the Revolutionary War by granting them land rather than paying them money. Pennsylvania limited warrants to around 300 acres. Land speculators and those who wanted to build a larger holding of land had to work the system. This was likely how Cpt. Boal acquired ownership of 4,000 acres of land in the Springfield area.

In 1789, Cpt. Boal settled in Centre County, Pennsylvania, on his 4,000-acre tract of land. Here, he built a portion of the Boal Mansion, although he never occupied the mansion. In 1798, his son, David Boal, Jr., emigrated from Ireland to the area. He added onto the Boal mansion and occupied it as a residence. As the area began to grow, the western end of town became known as Boalsburg. At that time, Springfield and Boalsburg were two different settlements.

Oak Hall dates back to a large piece of property surveyed in the warrantee name of Benjamin Bayless with letters of patent granted to Samuel Wallis. In 1768 Wallis sold the land to Reuben Haines, who in turn, about 1800, sold it to George McCormick, Sr. George McCormick, Sr. is possibly the first settler of Oak Hall, but it is not known if he actually lived in the village.

McCormick is known in local history as a miller who was the first settler of Spring Mills before 1800. McCormick's name appears in the Ferguson Township assessments of 1801 (which would have included the Oak Hall area) as owner of a gristmill and a sawmill in Oak Hall. In 1811 McCormick sold a portion of his Oak Hall tract to his son, George McCormick, Jr., and a 132-acre portion to John Irvin, Sr. Two years later, McCormick's son sold his portion to Jacob Hubler. This portion may have included the gristmill and sawmill.

In 1820 Jacob Johnstonbaugh purchased Hubler's property at Oak Hall. As early as 1819, Johnstonbaugh was assessed for a gristmill and a sawmill in the township. These are likely the same gristmill and sawmill that had been built by George McCormick in 1801. Johnstonbaugh built a homestead beside Spring Creek about halfway between the Irwin Mansion and the present-day Hanson Quarry. This house, now called the Johnstonbaugh House, was in close proximity to Johnstonbaugh's gristmill and sawmill. It is not known if Jacob and his wife ever occupied the Johnstonbaugh House. Later these two mills are thought to have been purchased by C. Stem.

About ½ mile north of Oak Hall was the hamlet of Dale's Mills. Christian Dale and his family moved to Centre County in 1790 where he began farming. Eventually, Christian and his son Felix established a gristmill, a sawmill, a hemp mill, and a general store. Dale's Mills ceased to exist as a thriving community, probably in the late 1870s. All that remains of the once thriving community is the Felix Dale House and a barn.

In this brief narrative, a number of structures that are still standing and some that have been demolishes are described. This book is suited to a short driving tour through Boalsburg and along Boalsburg Pike from Boalsburg to Oak Hall to Dale's Mills and on to Lemont.

Driving instructions are given in *italics*.

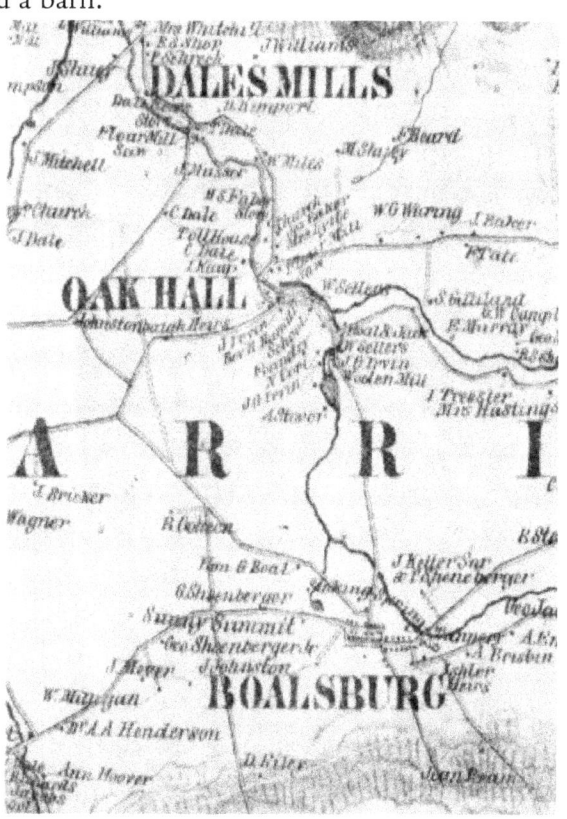

1861 Map of Boalsburg Pike

BUILDING PRACTICES

The villages of Springfield and Boalsburg as originally laid out by Andrew Stroup in 1809 was a rectangular grid configuration of quarter-acre lots. This layout was developed primarily between the years 1809 and 1850 and reflects the village's architectural, spatial, and cultural history during its growth to prominence as a major village in the early horse and wagon transit system. The structures within the original layout strongly suggest a pronounced European-British influence in urban planning, which is characterized by the use of such elements as the rectangular grid arrangement of streets, a public diamond or market area, narrow street widths, and the rather small, but closely situated spatial arrangement of houses. Within the main grid, multiple architectural types of structures evolved during the village's major growth period (1809-1850).

When settlers began to settle in the vicinity of Boalsburg, they sought natural resources with which to construct homes. It follows that many of the early residences in Boalsburg were log homes. The character of these homes has changed over the years as many have been expanded and have been remodeled. Today, exterior siding obscures all traces of the log character of most of these early log homes although some traces of the original log character may still be visible from the interior of a few homes.

The earliest structure that still exists in Boalsburg is the Boal Mansion. David Boal, Sr. built from stone what is now the kitchen area in circa 1789. The second-oldest structure in Boalsburg is probably the residence on the Gingrich Property. It was a log structure built circa 1801. The third-oldest structure still existing in Boalsburg is a log structure built by the Millers on Harmony Plantation. This structure was built in 1802, and today, it is called "The Tanner House."

Most of the very early homes built in Springfield-Boalsburg were log homes as it was the most readily available natural resource. Another early log structure was the David Boal, Jr.'s Boal Tavern built in 1804. This inn was in operation for 30+ years and a portion of the original structure remains. The Wolf Tavern is a two-story, five-bay, log structure that was built in 1834 on the northeast corner of the intersection of Main Street and Tennis Alley. It has been extensively remodeled. The Tait farmhouse was built in 1837, 1 mi. east of the village. The log part of the house rests on a foundation of stone and timber.

A second natural resource used in the construction of homes was limestone. Only a few homes in Boalsburg were built from stone. Two structures in Boalsburg of note built of stone are the Boalsburg Tavern and the George Stroup House. David Boal, Sr. built the kitchen part of the Boal Mansion from stone. The Zion Union Church in Boalsburg was also built of stone in 1827. It was often referred to as the "Old Stone Church." The stone foundation at the rear of the present-day Zion Lutheran Church is thought to be all that remains of the Zion Union Church. However, one need only drive a

Possible Remains of the "Old Stone Church."

short distance to Oak Hall and through the Spring Creek valley to Lemont to find several historic structures built from stone.

A few homes were built of brick. The earliest was the Hess House. It was built in 1830. The bricks were fired in the back yard. Another structure made from brick was the St. John's German Reformed Church (now the St. John's United Church of Christ), built in 1862. The brick for the Church were fired about 100 yds. westward on Pine Alley. The Zion Lutheran Church, built in 1868, was also built of brick.

In the first half of the 19th century, many buildings were wood frame structures. In the last half of the 19th century, there was much remodeling activity. Wooden siding was added to many homes.

ARCHITECTURAL STYLES

Springfield-Boalsburg exhibits three styles of architecture. The first was the log cabin style. Log cabins tended to be small, one-room, one-story, rectangular structures. This style was followed by the Georgian style, which appeared circa 1815. The Victorian style emerged in the later part of the 19th century.

Georgian architecture became popular in the early 19th century. It is characterized by simple symmetric geometry with classical lines and details, both inside and out. Common exterior materials included brick and stone (with stone quoins in the corners), clapboard, and shingle facing. Most structures have a simple rectangular footprint. There is often a medium pitched hip roof with a ridge pole parallel to the roadway. The exterior height usually has its highest point in the center. There are double hung windows without shutters. Windows are often large and regularly placed. Windows usually have nine or twelve panes per sash. In the interior, the fire place and hearth is often the main focus of rooms.

The Georgian style of architecture, with its long history in America, is among our country's most consistently popular styles. Admired for its symmetrical design, classic proportions, and decorative elements, it is directly tied to the work of the English architect Sir Christopher Wren. The peak of its popularity was during the time frame 1714-1830.

Typical floorplan of a Georgian style home: 3-bay center hall layout

During the late 1700s as the new country developed, there was a distinct lack of professional design advice, especially on the frontier. Therefore the, Georgian architecture in Centre County tended to differ somewhat from that in Philadelphia and other east coast cities.

Georgian architecture on the frontier tended to be characterized by symmetry, mathematical ratios, and simplicity. The figure above is a typical Georgian style floor plan for a 3-bay, center hall layout. All bays would have had the same ratio. The ratio shown is 1:2 regardless of the use of the room. Some of the earliest examples of Georgian architecture can be found in Boalsburg and between Boalsburg and Lemont, of which the George Stroup House (circa 1815), the Boalsburg (Duffy's) Tavern (1819), the Gen. James Irvin Mansion (1825), and the Felix Dale house (1823) are fine examples. Each has a simple hip roof with the ridge pole usually parallel to the roadway, sometimes with dormer windows, and a simple entry way (center or side hall). Symmetry is accented in the interior as there are bays based on geometric ratios. The footprints tend to be rectangular in shape. Symmetry is readily obvious. Additions and remodeling activities may have changed the original Georgian character of many of these buildings. Porches and window shutters would have been added a later time.

The schoolhouse at the juncture of Loop Road and Main Street exhibits many features of Georgian architecture. Another structure from this period is the John Hess House, a two-story, three-bay, brick structure built in 1826 on the southwest corner of the intersection of Main Street and Academy Street using a unique side hall plan.

Victorian architecture refers to several styles developed during the reign of Queen Victoria. It was popular in the last half of the 19th century. Victorian architecture is characterized by:

- Two to three stories. Victorian homes are usually large and imposing.
- Wood or stone exterior. The majority of Victorian styles use wood siding.
- Complicated, asymmetrical shape. Victorian homes tend to have wings and bays in many directions.
- Decorative trim. Commonly called "gingerbread," Victorian homes are usually decorated with elaborate wood or metal trim.
- Steep, multi-faceted roof or Mansard roof. Victorian homes often have steep, imposing rooflines with many gables facing in different directions.
- One-story porch. A large, wraparound porch with ornamental spindles and brackets.
- Towers. Some high-end Victorian homes are embellished with a round or octagonal tower with a steep, pointed roof.

No residence in Boalsburg has been identified as being a traditional Victorian home. Instead, many homes, especially log homes, were enlarged and remodeled during this period. During renovation, other rooms, siding, porches, window shutters, dormers, and decorative trim may have been added. These homes appear at first to be Victorian but they aren't.

The Peters House in Oak Hall shows some of early Victorian features. The Irvin Mansion exhibits some of these Victorian features that were added later. Thus, it is often difficult to identify the architectural style without a careful examination, both interior and exterior.

BOALSBURG TOUR

Proceed to the intersection of U. S. 322 and PA Route 45 east (to Centre Hall). The First National Bank is on the corner. There is a stoplight at this intersection. A right turn at this intersection is for Main Street into the village of Boalsburg. This is the starting point of the Boalsburg part of the tour. Take a right turn onto Main Street.

For orientation purposes, Tussey Mountain to your left is south and Mount Nittany to your right is to the north. Main Street in the direction of travel is west.

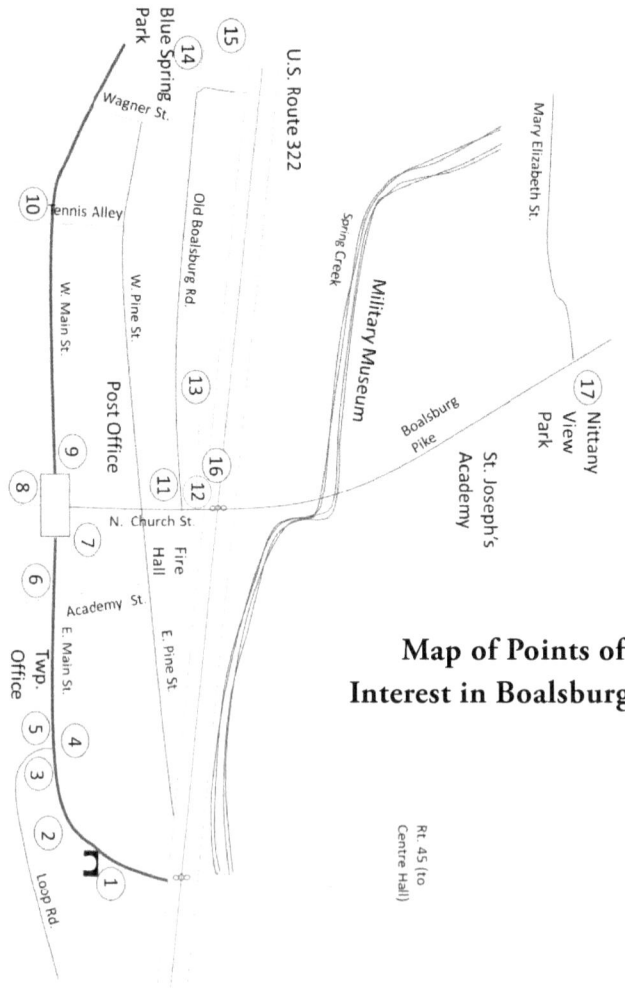

Map of Points of Interest in Boalsburg

1. Old Arch Bridge Behind the First National Bank

About 50 yards west on Main Street from the stop light is a tributary, and this is the site of the Old Arch Bridge. The Old Arch Bridge site is just beyond the First National Bank at the east end of Boalsburg. The bridge was probably built in the early 1800s although no exact date can be established. It no longer exists. It may have been part of the Springfield-Potter's Mills toll road. The tributary that flowed beneath this bridge originates from a spring on the north side of Loop Road directly across from the entrance to the Springfield Commons Housing Development. The east end of Boalsburg was originally known as Springfield and the town derived its early name from this spring. The tributary of this spring is unnamed.

2. The Power House of the Boalsburg Electric Company

As one begins to travel up the hill, the first building on the left is the power house of the Boalsburg Electric Company. In July 1914, the Boalsburg Electric Company was formed. Thus, Boalsburg became a part of the surge in America that had begun to utilize technology to generate electricity. It was recognized by villagers that small-scale hydropower systems could capture the energy in flowing water and convert it into cheap, clean electricity. Following successful litigation with the State College Water Company over water rights, a small hydroelectric plant was constructed in close proximity to where the tannery had been located and just east of the Boalsburg Heritage Museum. Water to generate electricity came from Galibreth Gap. The power generated was limited. Electricity was turned on around dusk and tuned off about 10:00 p.m.

With the coming of electricity, electric motors, lathes, etc., more and more items were made using standardized parts and components. Standardization made assembly lines practical. On the local level, standardization and mass production meant there was a greatly decreased demand for carriage shops and blacksmith shops.

3. The Sweet House

The next building on the left is the Sweet House. The Sweet House was built in 1825. The lot is thought to have been originally owned by John and Catherine Miller and sold to Michael Jack in 1804. Jack dug tan yard vats before selling the lot to William Murray, whose tannery had been located at the top of Mt. Nittany in 1801. Murray moved his tannery to Springfield in circa 1804. The Tannery operated at this location until near the end of the 19th century. Today, the Sweet House is the home of the Boalsburg Heritage Museum.

4. Boal Tavern

On the right side of Main Street stands the remains of the Boal Tavern. David Boal, Jr. built the Boal Tavern in 1804. In addition to a place to get food and drink, the Boal Tavern provided overnight accommodations and stables for the horses. It is improbable that the tavern would have been built unless the stagecoach was operating. So one can reasonably assume stagecoach operations began circa 1804. The tavern is thought to have operated until about the time of the economic "Panic of 1837."

5. Boalsburg's First Schoolhouse

Across Main Street on the south side opposite the Boal Tavern is a white house thought to be the first schoolhouse in Boalsburg. When Andrew Stroup laid out the village in 1809, he reserved several lots for schoolhouses. In 1810, a school was built on the southwestern corner of the intersection of Loop Rd. and Main St.

The structure that occupies this site is thought to be the original school building. It has many characteristics of Georgian Architecture, a style that was popular in the early 1800s. Further, it has many features common to other one-room schoolhouses in the area.

The next landmark is Academy Street. It is only a short distance up Main Street west of the Harris Township Office building.

6. The Hess House

On the southwest corner of Main Street and Academy Street stands the Hess House. It is one of only a handful of brick homes in the village of Boalsburg. It was built by John Hess in 1826 . The Hess house is a Georgian style home with a unique side entrance. The bricks were fired in the back yard. The Victorian Porch was added later. The side entrance may have been part of the porch addition. Many of the fine features of the original house have been preserved.

Continue proceeding a short distance westward to the village diamond.

7. Boalsburg Tavern

As you enter the diamond, on your right (north), is an imposing stone structure called Duffy's Tavern.

It was built in 1819 by Col. James Johnson and was known then as the Boalsburg Tavern. It was a favorite stop for the gentry class on the stagecoach. The tavern provided food and drink, overnight accommodations, and stables for the horses.

Col. Johnson and his wife, Hannah, lived in the Col. Johnson house which is diagonally across the diamond in the center of town. From his home, Col. Johnson could oversee the construction of the tavern.

The Boalsburg Tavern is of Georgian style architecture. It has a simple hipped roof with dormers. The ridge pole is parallel to the roadway. The front entrance is simple. The original structure was a three bay, center hall design.

The Tavern burned in 1934 and stayed dormant for three years thereafter. It was purchased for $500 and restored by Billy Winsor.

8. Col. Johnson House

Across the Diamond on its southern side is the Col. Johnson House. The Col. Johnson House dates to the early 1800s. It was built before the Boalsburg Tavern was built because it is said that Col. Johnson monitored the construction of the Tavern from his residence.

The residence is Georgian Style Architecture with a side hall entrance. The porch, a Victorian style feature, was added later.

Proceed westward to the edge of the diamond.
Continue to travel in a westerly direction about 50 yds.

9. George Stroup House

About 50 yds. or less beyond the diamond on the right (north) stands a small, two story stone structure called the George Stroup House. The lot where this stone house is built was one of the earliest lots sold by Andrew Stroup from his original layout of Springfield-Boalsburg in 1809. The lot was sold to George Stroup in 1810. There is no record of when this house was built. But it is one of the oldest homes in Boalsburg. The style of this house is Georgian, three bay, side hall. It has a hipped roof, and a ridge pole parallel to the roadway, which is typical English custom. This is one of the few residences in Boalsburg that is built of stone. Except for the addition in the back and the window shutters, it would appear that this structure has under gone few changes since it was built in circa 1815.

Continue to proceed in a westerly direction for another 50 yds. to Tennis Alley.

10. The Gingrich Property

Traveling westerly on Main Street, one shortly comes to Tennis Alley. On the southwest corner of this intersection is the Gingrich Property. After the property was sold to Christian Gingrich in the mid-1800s, it has been referred to as the Gingrich Property.

Gingrich Property.

The residence on the Gingrich Property on West Main Street was a log house and was built there circa 1800 by Isaac Womer. It is likely the second oldest residence still standing in Springfield/Boalsburg.

Mr. Womer was a saddler whose shop was located across Main Street from his residence. Mr. Womer made hand-cut and hand-sewn harnesses of leather he purchased from the tannery located at the eastern end of the village. A barn and ice house are still on the property.

Continue westward on Main St. to Wagner St. (about 150 yds.). Turn right (north). Go about 50 yds. and make the first right turn on Pine St. Go eastward past the post office and turn left (north) on N. Church St. Head north for about 50 yds..

11. St. John's United Church of Christ

About 50 yds. north of Pine St. on the left (west) stands a brick church.

Built in 1862, this was the third church building constructed in Boalsburg. Formerly called the German Reformed Church, it is now part of the United Church of Christ. The brick for the church were fired at the end of Pine Alley, about 100 yds. to the west.

The church is home to the Dürner organ, which was the first pipe organ in Centre County. It was built by Charles F. Dürner of Quakertown, PA who is now recognized as one of the finest American organ makers of the 19th century. An organ recital is given every Memorial Day.

Turn left heading west on Old Boalsburg Road. The turn is between the two churches.

12. Zion Union Church and Zion Lutheran Church

Immediately after you turn left, on your right (north) is the site of the Zion Union Church, often called the Old Stone Church. It was built in 1825-1827. The Zion Union Church and was home to the Congregations of the St. John's German Reformed Church and the Zion Lutheran Church from 1827 to 1862. The Church building was demolished in 1868 when the present Zion Lutheran Church was built on the same site.

In August 1862, students from the Boalsburg Academy met in the Old Stone Church and organized Company G of the 148th Pennsylvania Volunteers. They fought in the bloody Civil War battles of Antietam, Gettysburg, and Spotsylvania Court House.

13. Boalsburg Cemetery

The Boalsburg cemetery is believed to date back to circa 1827. The cemetery contains the graves of veterans from every war America has fought through the Vietnam War.

14. The Boal Mansion

After you pass the cemetery, you will come to two pilons that denote that you are entering the private Boal property. Looking diagonally to your left is the Boal Mansion. The Boal Mansion is the oldest structure in Boalsburg.

David Boal, Sr., an Irish emigrant, moved to the area in 1789 and built the first part of the mansion. He never lived in the mansion. Today, this first part of the mansion serves as the kitchen area. The mansion has been added onto twice, by David Boal, Jr, and by Theodore Boal.

15. Columbus Chapel

Theodore Boal's wife was related to Christopher Columbus. When her Aunt died, she inherited the Christopher Columbus family castle in Asturias, Spain. To make his wife feel at home in Boalsburg, Theodore Boal built a stone structure near the Boal Mansion, and after the World War I, he had the contents of the family castle in Spain shipped across the Atlantic, and set up in the stone structure (now called the Columbus Chapel) exactly as it had been set up in Spain. The chapel contents date from the 15th century and feature centuries worth of Columbus family history. One of the highlights is a sea chest that was owned by Christopher Columbus himself. Looking diagonally to the right, one can see the Chapel.

Heading east on Old Boalsburg Rd., proceed past the cemetery to Church Street (back-track) and turn left (north) towards the stop light.

16. Memorial Day Commoration Statue

Once you have passed the Church on your left, make a left turn into the cemetery. Looking diagonally to the right, one can see the statue of three ladies commorating the first Memorial Day.

In the fall of 1864, Emma Hunter, Elizbeth Meyer, and Sophie Keller went to the Boalsburg Cemetery to decorate the grave of Emma's father, Dr. Reuben Hunter. While decorating his grave, it was suggested that it would be appropriate to decorate the grave of a every soldier from the Civil War buried there, particularly members of the 148th Regiment of the Pennsylvania Volunteers, of which there were many. Thus, the tradition of decorating graves on Decoration Day (as it was called then) began.

Exiting the cemetery, turn left (north) and keep straight through the stop light, heading north.. Once you cross U. S. 322, you will be on Boalsburg Pike. Go about ¾mi. just beyond the crest of the hill at Pine Tree St. Mount Nittany will be visible in the distance. On your right is Nittany View Park. Just opposite the park is Mary Elizabeth St.

17. Boalsburg Air Depot

In 1929, Sherm Lutz opened an air depot in Boalsburg atop the hill between Boalsburg and Oak Hall, where "the pine tree" stood. Looking to the east, the end of the runway is still visible from Nittany View Park. Lutz was the first person to deliver the mail via air to the area.

This is the end of the Boalsburg part of the tour.
If you wish to transition to the Oak Hall part of the tour, go down Mary Elizabeth St. to Warner Blvd about ¼ mi. At the stop light, turn right and go beneath the U. S. 322 bridge on the bypass..
The bridge is the starting point of the second part of the tour.

OAK HALL-DALE'S MILLS TOUR

The upper third (southerly third) of the village of Oak Hall was taken by PADOT in the late 1960s to construct the Oak Hall and Boalsburg interchange of the State College bypass. This part of the tour begins as one passes beneath the bypass bridge on Warner Blvd.

Begin this part of the tour at the U.S 322 bypass bridge and travel about 100 yds. northward towards Lemont.

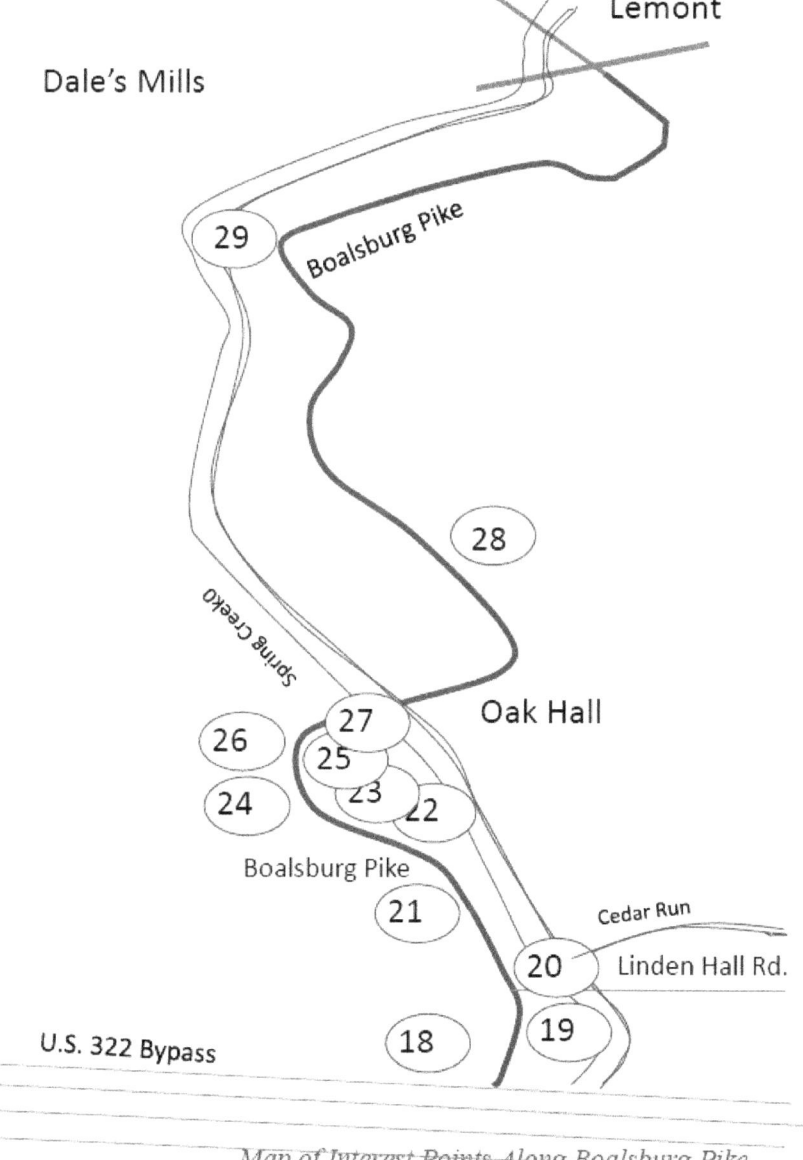

Map of Interest Points Along Boalsburg Pike

18. Rye-Ho Woolen Factory

Immediately after passing under the bridge is a grassy knoll on the left. (west).

This is the site of the former Rye-Ho Woolen Factory, owned by James Irwin. This mill was demolished circa 1967 when the bypass was built. There was a small pond associated with the factory. Spring Creek was rerouted and the pond was also demolished. There are no remains.

19. Stover's General Store

On the right east) side of the road (east) set back from the road about 50 yds., are the remains of a general store owner by A & D Stover. It supposedly became a general store in the 1890s. It is also alleged to have been a tavern. When a Post Office was established in 1886, it was located in this building.

Proceed to Linden Hall Road. You are now on Boalsburg Pike.

20. Foundry and Blacksmith Shop

A foundry shop was once located on the right (east) at the intersection of Linden Hall Road and Boalsburg Pike. A blacksmith shop was located on the south side of the foundry. The foundry office, which still exists, was located on the north side. The foundry specialized in tools for the logging industry. The foundry likely went out of business with the demise of the logging industry.

Continue traveling north in the direction of Lemont.

21. Upper Schoolhouse

About halfway between the foundry site and the curve, on the left (west), is the site of the upper schoolhouse. The upper schoolhouse in Oak Hall dates back to the early 1800s. It is known that the Congregations of St. John's German Reformed and the Zion Lutheran Churches started worshipping here around 1820 prior to building the Zion Union Church in Boalsburg (No. 12). The upper schoolhouse no longer exists.

22. Stone Barn

Around the curve on the right (east) is a stone barn built by Gen. James Irvin circa 1825. An unusual degree of refinement is evidenced in the regularity of the window placement and, especially in the introduction of a Palladian window (ventilator) at the top of the gable end facing the mansion. The barn has a hipped roof and ridge pole that is roughly parallel to the roadway.

23. Irvin Mansion

The Irvin mansion was built by General James Irvin around 1825. Gen. Irvin was one of the most prominent citizens of Centre County until his death in 1862. He was a Major General in the 10th Division of the Pennsylvania Militia. He served in Congress (1843-1845) and unsuccessfully ran for Governor in 1847. He was a renowned ironmaster. At one time or another he owned seven iron furnaces in Centre County, including Centre Furnace.

The Georgian style mansion is a 2-½ story dwelling and was built in 1825 using a five bay, center hall floor plan. The exterior stone was chiseled to yield a smooth exterior finish. A Victorian front porch and Victorian dormers were added later.

24. Lower Schoolhouse

Across Boalsburg Pike (west) from the Irwin Mansion is the site of the Lower Schoolhouse. It was a one-room schoolhouse built in 1879, and it served the area until 1937.

25. The Irvin Mill

The Irvin Mill was built by Gen. Irvin in 1823 a hundred yards north of the Irwin mansion and on the east side of the road. It was originally built as a brick mill, but most writings refer to the Irwin Mill as a gristmill. One writing refers to it as a woolen mill and cites a date of 1836. After the death of Gen Irvin in 1862, there were numerous owners. By 1874, the mill was known as the Stem Bros. Grist Mill. The mill burned in 1880. When the mill closed in 1948, it was being used as a gristmill. The history of the usage of the mill cannot be established with certainty. All that remains of the Irwin Mill is its stone foundation.

The accompanying figure shows the back of the Irvin mill and the pond directly behind the Irwin Mansion which was used to assure a continuous supply of water to the mill. The remains of the dam can still be seen. The pond was a popular destination for ice skaters in the winter. The mill owners also used the pond as a source for extra income by selling ice.

26. Peters' House

Opposite the Irwin Mill is the Benjamin Peters' House. It was built around 1860 and is a fine example of the sort of dignified country residences that were being built in the area around the time of the Civil War. Although it doesn't rival the earlier Irvin Mansion, the Peters' house nevertheless conveys a clear image of refinement. The house suggests a middleclass owner who could now reflect status with early Victorian design features.

27. The Johnstonbaugh House

A short distance further on Boalsburg Pike, just before the bridge over Spring Creek and on the right (east), stands the Johnstonbaugh House.

In 1820 Jacob Johnstonbaugh purchased the Hubler property at Oak Hall. As early as 1819, he had been assessed for a gristmill and a sawmill in the township. He built a homestead beside Spring Creek about halfway between the Irwin Mansion and the present-day Hanson Quarry. This house, called the Johnstonbaugh House, was in close proximity to his gristmill and sawmill. It is not known if Jacob and his wife occupied the Johnstonbaugh House.

Proceed to Hanson Quarry.

28. Albright Church

Little is known about the Albright Church, and what has been written cannot be collaborated. It is questionable if the Albright Church ever existed. What little has been written is summarized below.

As early as the 1820s, the Albrecht's (Albright's) People came to Centre County as a loosely organized church founded by a preacher named Jacob Albrech (Albright). It was later called the Evangelical Association. This church underwent various mergers and schisms and today is a part of the United Methodist Church.

There is no written record of a church ever being built in Oak Hall, although the location of the Albright Church is recorded in The Atlas of Centre County by Pomeroy & Co. in 1874. It has been written that "Surely a building was planned at Oak Hall . . ." as there were many Evangelicals living in Oak Hall. Whether a church was actually built or when is unknown.

If there was ever an Evangelical Church built in Oak Hall as noted by The Atlas of Centre County and it still exists it may be located on the present-day Hanson Quarry site, on the right-hand side (east) of Boalsburg Pike while in route to Lemont. Here sits a simple, stone structure that appears to be used by the quarry operation as an office or as a storage area. The building has a hipped roof and ridge pole that is parallel to the roadway. It was obviously not built as a residence.

Proceed northward to Dale's Mills (about ¼ mile shy of Lemont).

29. Felix Dale House

About ½ mile further along Boalsburg Pike from Oak Hall and about ¼ mile shy of Lemont, is a stone house on the left (west) called the Felix Dale House. The Felix Dale house was completed in 1823. Felix Dale operated a gristmill and a sawmill. He later added a hemp mill and general store. The mills were located in the open field beyond the barn. The area became known as the hamlet of Dale's Mills.

The Felix Dale family were affluent residents of Centre County. Felix's father, Christian, helped establish transportation routes throughout the County. He oversaw the construction of General Benner's road (now the Benner Pike), and he petitioned the state government for a road that would run from Dale's Mills to the General Benner's road. The stone house was a Georgian style house. It was a five bay, side hall floor plan. It has a gabled roof. The exterior of the structure has been chiseled for a smooth surface. The corners of the house are constructed with larger blocks. There are two front doors. There are many unique architectural features about the Felix Dale house, and its architecture is likely why it was listed on the National Register of Historic Places in 1982.

Proceed ¼ mi. north on Boalsburg Pike to Lemont to conclude the tour.

OTHER POINTS OF INTEREST

Between Boalsburg and Lemont, there are five sites listed on the National Registry of Historic Places. These are:

- Boalsburg Historic District
- Felix Dale House (Dale's Mills)
- Oak Hall Historic District
- The Boal Mansion (Boalsburg)
- The Hill House (Boalsburg)

In total, there are 63 sites in Centre County on the National Registry. Other nearby sites listed on the national registry are:

- Centre Furnace Mansion
- Egg Hill Church
- Gen. John Thompson House
- Lemont Historic District
- Linden Hall Historic District

BIBLIOGRAPHY

Corter, R., and M. Riley. Boalsburg: An American Village. The Boalsburg Village Conservancy, Boalsburg, PA, 36 pp. 1986.

Fredericks, G., D. Hatch, P. Thomas and R. Thomas. The History of St. John's United Church of Christ—The First 200 Years. October, 2017.

Hermann, Michael. 1874 Oak Hall Mills Map, 1994.

Hermann, Michael. 1884 Map recreated from Atlas of Center County by Beaun Nichols. A. Pomeroy & Co., Philadelphia, 1874.

Holden, Harold. The Chapel of Christopher Columbus and the Boal Mansion: The Story of an American Heritage. Columbus Chapel and Boalsburg Estate Society, 1956.

http://en.wikipedia.org/wiki/Jacob_Albright

https://en.wikipedia.org/wiki/National_Register_of_Historic_Places_listings_in_Centre_County,_Pennsylvania

http://millpictures.com/mills.php?millid=5021

http://www.bing.com/search?q=boalsburg+inn+restaurant&FORM=QSRE1

http://www.hgtv.com/design/home-styles/victorianarchitecture

http://www.livingplaces.com/PA/Centre_County/College_Township/Oak_Hall_Historic_District.html

http://www.livingplaces.com/PA/Centre_County/Harris_Township/Boal_Mansion.html

Linn, John Blair. History of Centre and Clinton Counties, PA, Philadelphia, PA, Louis H. Everts, 1883.

Margalgel, Myrtle. History of Boalsburg. (September 28, 1938-March 20, 1939). In Centre Daily Times: State College, PA.

McElhoe, J. S. A Small Stream Changed a Village: First Electricity in Boalsburg. Crandell Publishing Company, State College, PA, 2018.

McElhoe, J. S. Village Craftsmen. Boalsburg Heritage Museum, 340 Main Street, Boalsburg, PA, 2018.

Nichols, B. Atlas of Centre County. Pomeroy & Co., Philadelphia, PA, 1874.

Ramsey, Gregory, Centre County Historic Restoration Project, Oak Hall Historic District, nomination document, 1979, National Park Service, National Register of Historic Places, Washington, D.C.

Stan Smith, Informal Conversations. April, 2018.

Thomas, Michael J. Centre County: From Its Earliest Settlement to the Year 1915, Pennsylvania State University Libraries, 1915.

Thomas, R., The Founding of Boalsburg—The Stagecoach Era, 1774-1855. Boalsburg Heritage Museum, 340 Main Street, Boalsburg, PA, 2018.

Thomas, R., A History of Boalsburg, Oak Hall, and Linden Hall, Pennsylvania, Mt. Nittany Press, Lemont, PA, 2020.

Thomas, R., A History of Boalsburg, Pennsylvania, Mt. Nittany Press, Lemont, PA, 2020.

www.ingramcontent.com/pod-product-compliance
Lightning Source LLC
LaVergne TN
LVHW011900060526
838200LV00054B/4441